Zero to Fifty

Drive On.
Kate Lake

Zero to Fifty

A LIFETIME IN THE DRIVER'S SEAT

A MEMOIR by Kate Lake

ALGONQUIN BOOKS OF CHAPEL HILL 2003

Published by
ALGONQUIN BOOKS OF CHAPEL HILL
Post Office Box 2225
Chapel Hill, North Carolina 27515-2225

a division of
WORKMAN PUBLISHING
708 Broadway
New York, New York 10003

Library of Congress Cataloging-in-Publication Data
Lake, Kate
     Zero to fifty: a lifetime in the driver's seat.— 1st ed.
       p. cm.
     ISBN 1-56512-342-5
     1. Motor vehicles—United States—Anecdotes.   2. Popular culture—United States.   3.
Lake, Kate, 1953– I. Title.
     TL23 .L35   2003
     937.92'092—dc21
     [B]   2002033271

10 9 8 7 6 5 4 3 2 1
First Edition

For Patsy

I must have been two or three. I was standing on the sidewalk in the sunshine. My parents' Plymouth was in the driveway. It was large and gray and reassuring. This is the first thing I remember.

Everyone I know has a car story. They usually have something to do with the best and the worst of life: trips to emergency rooms, first loves, bad fights, road trips, and wrong turns. We move through life in our cars. In our stories we reveal ourselves as, say, the sort of person who would ignore all logic and common sense and buy the Fiat convertible just because we like the person we think we become behind the wheel. That's the way it went with me anyway. And that's why I wrote a love story about the wheels that have carried me here.

Zero to Fifty

1947 Plymouth Sedan

My parents came out to L.A. from McAlester, Oklahoma, in a 1947 Plymouth. They loaded up their car with paintings and poetry and turned left on Route 66, headed west. My mother's name was Patsy, my dad's was Bob. There is a photo of them standing in front of the Plymouth somewhere on Mulholland Drive. Hollywood is at their feet and they're both smiling and looking a little wild.

The Plymouth was with us for a long time. Patsy learned to drive it in the early sixties—doing figure eights in the Sears parking lot while my sister, Leslie, and I clung to the velveteen rope on the back of the front seat, convinced we were going to die. After each lesson we'd stop off at the Venetian Room for drinks. Patsy would bring us out a couple of Shirley Temples before repairing to the bar for something stiffer. We'd stay in the car playing with our dolls and double-daring each other to release the emergency brake to see what would happen.

1962 Ford Country Squire Station Wagon

The Albrights down the street were my idea of the perfect family. Mr. Albright looked like Fred MacMurray. Their car was every eight-year-old's dream machine. It was white with paneled side stripes done up in fake wood grain, and fabulous brown-and-white leatherette seats with little cowboy brands stamped into them. It was the ultimate urban cowpoke accessory. I'd put on my holsters and the little red cowgirl hat with "Katie" embroidered across the crown that I'd received for my birthday. When Mr. Albright parked the car in the driveway after work, I'd get behind the wheel and pretend to be chasing down bad guys, while the smaller kids took the rear suicide seat and covered me from behind.

1961 Dark Blue Lincoln Continental Stretch Limo

It was *Televisión Español* hour in my fourth-grade classroom. The woman on the screen was saying "Buenos dias muchachos" and smiling expectantly at the class. We were supposed to say "Buenos dias, maestra" back at her. But she vaporized and Chet Huntley appeared with the news that Kennedy had been shot. For weeks after that, we watched replays of the long dark convertible, flags fluttering, moving slowly through Dallas. Something is wrong. Jackie is reaching back over the trunk. People are running toward the car. The limo is everywhere, before the shots, after the shots, during. Screaming into the emergency room entrance, and later carrying the coffin to the plane. It probably wasn't the same car, but it began to seem like an accomplice to murder. My mom's mom died the same day in Oklahoma. My parents were big Kennedy fans and I was never sure whom Patsy was grieving for most.

1964 AMC Rambler

Bob left us sometime in the mid-sixties and then Patsy bought the Rambler.
These days it's a cult classic, but it was an embarrassment then. As I grew
older, my desire for independence was tempered by my desire to appear
cool. Patsy taught me to drive and stuck a hatpin in the sun visor "in case
I ever needed it." That was her way of explaining wickedness in the world.
None of us was a very good driver and there were accidents. Patsy would take
the Rambler down to Earl ("I will paint any car . . .") Scheib for a yearly
$29.95 paint job—some years pale pink, some years baby blue, dents intact.
It always looked new and abused at the same time. On weekends, I'd drive out
to the desert listening to Wolfman Jack on the radio. I'd get out to where there
was nothing, pull over to the side of the road, and walk a mile or so until it
was very quiet: just the little pink/blue Rambler shimmering in the heat by
the road, and me.

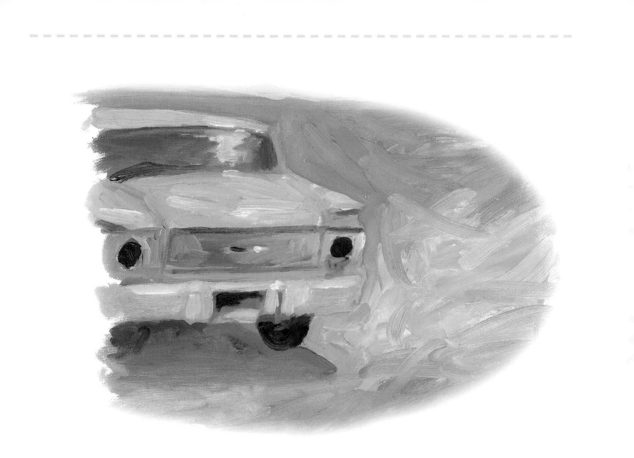

1957 Cadillac Ragtop

My father would resurface occasionally with a new wife or a new car
in tow. Once it was a yellow Cadillac convertible and a woman named
Marcia. The car looked like a Rose Parade float. Marcia wore sunglasses
and a scarf like Gina Lollobrigida. The Cadillac had big fins and a
red leather interior. We went out for ice cream and tried to appear
unconcerned while Bob and Marcia argued about when he would return
us. I didn't see him for years after that, until I heard Marcia had run off
with some guy named Ramón. Even back then my sister, Leslie, and
brother, Evan, and I would try to remember when it was exactly that
Bob left us, but we all had different recollections.

First Date

A girl I knew in junior high needed a date for her boyfriend's cousin and asked me. Her mother would only let her go out if it was a double date. The cousin had a mustache and was in the navy and drove a yellow Mustang with racing stripes, black bucket seats, and a four-on-the-floor. We were supposed to go see something with Hayley Mills in it, but instead we drove to the El Monte Drive-In and watched *Valley of the Dolls*. The girl and her boyfriend were in the backseat going at it. Sailor-boy put his arm on my shoulder and then let it fall to my forearm and then my knee. It was a good thing there were bucket seats. I don't remember much about the movie except Dionne Warwick's singing *Gotta get, gonna get, off from this ride.*

1964 Volkswagen Beetle

I did two years of food service after school at a hot dog place called Der Wienerschnitzel. There was a big sign on the wall that said IF YOU HAVE TIME TO LEAN, YOU HAVE TIME TO CLEAN. I was reading a lot of George Orwell at the time, so it all sort of added up. At the end of my shift my friends would pick me up—sometimes in their mom's Hornet or, if they were lucky and rich, in their own car. We'd head up to the foothills and smoke pot and make up bad poetry while the lights of the city twinkled and the blurry line we knew was the ocean darkened and disappeared. A boy named Eric, who looked vaguely like Peter Tork of the Monkees, taught me to drive stick shift in his VW. With *Forever Changes* in the tape player, and Eric—stoned and stoic—riding shotgun, I'd lurch around empty backstreets in third gear. I finally figured out how to drive it, but Eric never got laid like he hoped he might.

Vauxhall Victor

I had a friend named Cathy who drove a Vauxhall her dad had fixed up for her. It looked like a Chevy Bel-Air squashed to about three-quarter size. Cathy would pick me up after my shift at Der Wienerschnitzel and we'd cruise up and down the boulevards, hanging, listening to the radio, and making hostile chitchat about people we hated. Even though I smelled like hot dog grease and cigarettes, that car made me feel very mod.

Patsy's habits were beginning to get the best of her and she was in and out of the hospital a lot. We fought about everything—her drinking, my friends, money, drugs. When it got too crazy, the first one to reach them would grab the keys to the Rambler and peel out of the driveway, brakes squealing all the way down the street. I don't know where Patsy went when she got the keys. I just drove around.

1957 Chevrolet Nomad

I lost my virginity in the back of my boyfriend's blue Chevy wagon. A summer job near Big Sur, Van Morrison cycling endlessly in the eight-track stereo. At the time it seemed pretty damned romantic. I had a big crush on that guy, but after that summer I never saw him again.

Where I'm from, white kids drove sleds like the Nomad, or pimped-out GTOs if they were jocks. The black kids drove Chryslers and old Caddies with lace jobs, tuck-and-roll upholstery, and "Crystal Blue Persuasion" in spirit-writing on the back window. Hispanic kids drove low-rider Volkswagens, so cherried out with hydraulics they could make the car mambo in the street. You can understand my mixed feelings about Patsy's Rambler. The Nomad ran fine as long as you kept pouring water into the radiator. That summer we took turns driving Highway 1 from Monterey to L.A., stopping every fifteen miles or so to pop the hood and take care of business. That's the beauty of those old Chevies: They're just pure car and you don't have to be a motorhead to know what makes them run.

Vicky's Volkswagen Van

Vicky lived in another part of town but somehow we ended up palling around together. She had a brand new blue VW van that became, for my circle of friends, the party machine. It took us to the beach, to parties in Hollywood canyons, to skanky hippie pads in the hills, and, once, to Yuma, Arizona, and the edge of the Colorado River at dawn. Peace symbols swung from the rearview mirror and the bumper glistened with subversive stickers. This was not yet a cliché. We picked up every hitchhiker we saw, Sufi dancer and psycho killer alike, seeking news from the world we were moving toward. There's a time in life when a car and a road offer a kid a peek at what it is to be up and grown. On the trip to Yuma the engine caught fire. We pulled into a gas station and they pulled an engine out of another VW and replaced it.

KATE LAKE

My Friends All Drive Porsches I

My pal Cathy's cousin Dan spent his summers fishing in Alaska, leaving his '64 Porsche 356 convertible in Cathy's driveway. The keys were hanging on a hook by the back door in case it needed to be moved in an emergency. Cathy and I spent one morning coming up with a list of emergencies, but in the end it was just a crime of opportunity.

Route 2 leaves Los Angeles near Pasadena and climbs to the top of the San Gabriel mountains. At the summit, you can look west to the Pacific Ocean and east to the Mojave. In Dan's Porsche, we made the traverse from sea to desert in record time. Outside of Pearblossom, we switched and I took the wheel. The road flattened into the distance in a continuous line. I shifted the car into fourth and floored it. Jackrabbits skittered back into the ocotillo and creosote bush. Cathy laughed and howled at the sky like a wildcat. That afternoon was very, very good.

We were stopped by the CHP outside of Barstow and hauled in. Dan declined to press charges. The officer hung around after our hearing and volunteered to drive the Porsche back to L.A. himself.

My Friends All Drive Porsches II

Like many a big-boned white girl with Southern roots, I was a huge, *huge* Janis Joplin fan. My girlfriend Candy and I hitchhiked up to the Bay Area in 1969 to see her play. *Cheap Thrills* had just come out. After the show, we found a place to crash by asking around. I really wanted to kiss Candy, and the rumor that Joplin was bisexual was the excuse I needed. Candy didn't go for it. Years later, at an auto show, I saw Joplin's car. It was not a Mercedes Benz but a 1965 Porsche Cabriolet sort of like the one I stole except painted in a wild-ass pop mural of primary colors with pictures of her and Big Brother. I like to think about that pissed-off Wild Girl from Port Arthur and her Fuck You car.

Kesey's Bus and My Oregon Adventure

At seventeen, I left L.A. and headed north, ending up in Springfield, Oregon. I sent Patsy a letter saying I would stay awhile but I'd send money, and then I began life as a free-range grown-up. My travel partner was the brother of the girl who made the yogurt for the guy who ran the Creamery and was the brother of Ken Kesey. We camped out in her house and I went to work at the Creamery pouring fruit into little plastic containers. I had read *The Electric Kool-Aid Acid Test* and felt blessed to have arrived at the very font of all hippiedom. Kesey didn't like visitors, but I distributed the last of my travel pot to my hosts and won an invitation to the farm. The bus, Furthur, was there, parked next to the barn, forlorn and covered with blackberry vines. Dust to dust. The others spent the afternoon drinking gin and inhaling helium to make their voices sound funny. I sat and watched the bus for a while, then hitched a ride back to town.

1952 Willys Jeep Overland

After the Creamery, I landed a waitress job. I spent my first paycheck on a Jeep with a worthless Hurricane Six engine. I painted the dashboard yellow and decoupaged butterflies on it. When the head gasket blew, my new boyfriend replaced the little engine with a big truck motor. A new transmission, driveline, and rear end followed. We had to cut a two-foot-square hole in the floorboards to accommodate the new stick shift, and the rear end lifted the back of the Jeep so high, I couldn't see anything but sky in the rearview mirror.

One day I was driving downtown when the Jeep screeched to a halt. My long skirt was wrapped around the exposed driveline and I was naked from the waist down. A crowd gathered. My boyfriend fell out of the car because he was laughing so hard. It looked like a bad accident. Not long after that, the front end collapsed. The engine was just too much for it.

1948 Dodge Powerwagon

In those years my attraction to men was influenced by the cars they drove.
A form of autoeroticism, I guess. My new boyfriend, Sean, had a fine assortment
of wheels, including a Dodge Power Wagon and assorted vintage motorcycles.
He was a tall, rangy guy who spent most of his time tinkering on one machine
or another, his long legs sticking out from underneath this or that. It still gets
me a little hot.

The Power Wagon was the sort of vehicle you might use to launch a military
assault on your neighbors. In first gear you could drive up a vertical wall. When
some friends needed to get a large piece of machinery into a second-story office,
they rigged up a block and tackle and backed the Dodge down the street as a sort
of mobile winch. Today's SUVs pale in comparison.

1948 Indian Chief

The most beautiful motorcycle ever built was the 1948 Indian Chief. Poseurs are everywhere, but only the very lucky few have ever actually ridden one and fewer still can claim one as their own. I have a photo of Sean on his Indian surrounded by an awestruck hardcore biker gang called the Free Souls. It was a classic deep red with full-skirt fenders that made the bike look like the Queen of England on parade. It had a 74-cubic-inch twin engine with a suicide shift, twin tanks, chrome speedo, magneto, and fringed saddlebags attached behind the single tractor seat; the headlamp featured an ivory Bakelite auxiliary light in the shape of an Indian's head. He never let me ride it.

1948 Chevrolet Pickup

After the Jeep broke down I traded it and a sewing machine for this beautiful pickup truck. It had a sweet little straight six in it. I had city-girl daydreams of hauling hay and old motorcycles around. Patsy was having a difficult time back in L.A., so my little brother and sister came up to live with me that summer. We had fun running wild, pretending we were country kids. Leslie got a big crush on a biker named Mike, and Evan reveled in boyland, lighting small fires and torturing waterfowl. In September we packed up the truck and drove back down the coast, stopping every fifty miles so Les and Evan could trade places in the cab and get warm. I didn't know it, but it would be the last time we were all together.

KATE LAKE

1953 Matchless, 1960 Ducati

The Matchless was Sean's too. It had one large 500cc cylinder—some folks call those bikes "thumpers." If you're a girl and you're reading this and you've ridden one of these machines, I don't need to tell you what their particular charms are. The first time I tried to kick it over was in my front yard. I hadn't lined up the piston quite right and when I whomped on it, it threw me right over the handlebars. There were a bunch of guys sitting on the porch watching and they got a nice laugh out of that. I think they set the whole scenario up.

The Ducati was a gift. It was in three wood orange crates and came with a xeroxed manual. I kept it in my bedroom for a year before it disappeared.

1963 Norton Atlas

I love old bikes and I was particularly attracted to motorcycles that had only a slim chance of actually running. I think it was my survival instinct. I got this bike from a guy named Terry who had a pile of old Nortons in his backyard. Aficionados tend to dismiss the Atlas as a piece of crap, but it was seriously fast. We'd ride to the outskirts of town and race. I'd have the bike well over the posted limit and still in third gear, and then it would vibrate so terribly that something important—the exhaust pipes, for example—would fall off. A guy I know used to call bikes like these "80/20"s. Eighty part fix to twenty part ride. Sean and I broke up but I kept the Norton.

International Cab-Over Semi-Truck

I was trying to pick up some extra cash, so when a friend asked me whether I thought I could handle a semi-truck, I said, "Sure." We picked up stuff all the way down the interstate and then reversed direction and off-loaded it all back in Oregon. In Oakland, the trailer was unhooked and we'd drive the tractor into San Francisco. We'd park and catch a movie or find a bar and go dancing. The Hustle and the Bus Stop were hot. Truck driving wasn't particularly hard. Staying awake for long stretches was the main skill. Girl drivers were still pretty unusual. We didn't have a CB radio but you really didn't want to hear what the guys were saying anyway. I was beginning to get wind of the whole women's movement thing and I could tell by the way people looked at us that there was something bigger at stake. When it took too much time to find a gear, I felt I was letting everyone down. I didn't drive for long. The romance of truck driving is pretty short-lived.

1960-Something Isabella Borgward

I didn't go to college, but I learned to hang around campuses and absorb what I needed. Over at the University of Oregon, they had foreign films every Friday night. Fellini was my favorite: all those high cheekboned, scarved and shaded women with impossibly high heels and the handsome nervous men who picked them up in little Italian coupes. When I saw the Borgward . . . well, I look nothing like Fellini's Giulietta, but for a moment I heard music. I owned the Borgward for about a week. It needed a chain-type thingy to replace the one that ran the transmission, and I learned that this (and most) Borgward parts were generally unavailable. That's the problem with old foreign jobbies. To love a car like that, you've got to be a machinist or wealthy enough to keep one on retainer. I'd just go sit in it sometimes, running my hands over the dashboard with all its little metric doodads. Heaven.

1965 Dodge Dart Convertible

This was the car my little brother, Evan, was tinkering with the summer he died. It was an accident, but it didn't have anything to do with a car. Nobody ever knows what to do when a kid dies, where to put their hands or rest their eyes. My dad had resurfaced and he kept talking about the Dart and Evan. He'd given it to Evan and Evan had liked it and that was good. Dad asked me to take the Dart, to have something of Evan. It was a Special Edition ragtop with push-button transmission and power everything. I was always pouring automatic steering fluid or brake fluid or something into it. It was a lush. When I parked it, middle-aged men would gather around and make little purring noises. Guys really liked the car. I drove it off-road once and crunched a hole in the gas tank by driving over a rock. A logging truck stopped and the driver whittled a little plug out of wood and fixed it. I drove it like that for another year or so before it was stolen. My dad would ask me about the car whenever we talked and I didn't have the heart to tell him it was gone.

1948 Buick Woody Dynaflow Station Wagon

I was ready to leave town and I needed a vehicle I could tie mattresses and household goods to, and possibly live in if things didn't pan out. The Dynaflow had been sitting over by the railroad tracks for a couple of weeks with a hand-lettered FOR SALE sign in the window. I paid $300 and the guy threw in a case of engine sealant. He swore that it would solve the problem of the cracked block. Everyone has to have a car like this once—a car that takes your breath away. The Dynaflow was a yacht: the first automatic transmission, a silver bud vase on the dashboard that I always kept a rose or two in, and a sexy, thunderous engine. I could usually get about four ecstatic miles before it overheated and died. It would have had a hard time hitting the highway. I was working two jobs then— at a printing press during the day and as a janitor evenings. I had to wear a goofy smock. The people in the offices I cleaned would leave quarters on the desk to see if I would steal them and when that got to me, I'd remember the Dynaflow and think how much cooler I was.

1958 Chevy Wagon

A mechanic friend once told me: "I'm a bow-tie man till the day I die." I knew what he meant. Chevies: it's hard to kick the habit. I bought this from a woman I met walking down the street. She was young and had two small kids and needed money. I was dating a girl named Betsy, who wanted to move, so we packed the Chevy and headed for the big city. We broke up about twelve hours after we hit town but I had the car for years. A friend and I rebuilt the engine. It took a long time, and when it was done we were knocking back congratulatory beers when I noticed a little gear sitting on the bench. I had to take the engine apart and put it back together again. I haven't worked on a car since. People should do what they're good at and leave the rest to others.

1978 GMC School Bus

I found work in a print shop, but funds were tight so I took a second job driving a school bus, a position I was wholly unsuited for emotionally. My day started at 5:00 A.M. By 6:15 I was picking up sullen eighth-graders. I had a spiky haircut and a bad attitude, and I learned that unannounced application of the bus's compression brake was a useful form of behavior control. I did that for three years.

Not long after I moved, my mother died. She hadn't been well for a long time and Evan's death had pretty much done her in. At the cemetery in L.A., we read poems she had written and a friend of hers said she knew the end was coming when Patsy had to give up her car. I was a pissed-off, sorrowful mess. It took awhile, a long time after that, to get it together. Eventually, I started to see the balance. To see all the good stuff as well as the bad.

1973 Yamaha TXS 650CC Motorcycle

I eventually quit the print shop, enrolled in night school, and bought the Yamaha in order to save on gas. Fuel had soared into the 80¢-a-gallon range. For anyone who has owned a Norton, a Yamaha is many notches down on the coolness scale. Still, it had the advantage of running for prolonged periods of time—sometimes up to a month or two. I was beginning to develop a plan for my life, and reliable mobilization had become important. One year into my academic stint, a music magazine hired me. They thought I was hip with the motorcycle and all. Their motto was "Bands you've never heard of that have broken up by the time you read this." They gave me the night shift, so I left school.

1977 Toyota Celica

After Evan and Patsy died, my dad, my sister, and I decided to drive to Oklahoma to see the grandparents and try to get to know one another better. A healing reunion sort of thing. The Celica was Bob's idea of a midlife-crisis car. He had a CB in it and spent most of the trip drinking Jack Daniels out of the bottle and talking trash with the long-haulers. At a truck stop in Tecumcari, I got out and walked over to the Greyhound bus station. I had a strong feeling that I was going to die if I stuck it out in that car. Leslie came and found me and talked me back. Bob had fallen asleep, so I took the wheel, hitting the Indian Nation Tollway at dawn, crossing the meandering Canadian River a dozen times before pulling into my grandparents' driveway. Later on, we all went out to eat at Joe's Place near the highway. After dinner we ambled out to my grandparents' Buick Skylark. Granddad put his arm around me and squeezed gently. The cicadas roared in the pecan trees.

1965 Ford Falcon Station Wagon

Julie was a Montana cowgirl who drove large road-building equipment like graders and rollers, a career she took up after she got tired of being a lawyer. We met in 1978 and began a wild affair that would eventually mellow into a lifelong friendship. She worked all over the state and found girlfriends in every port. But I was smitten. Once, in a fit of jealous insanity, I rode the Yamaha over a mountain pass in an early blizzard to confront her. When I arrived, I had to sit for an hour in an IHOP before I could uncurl my fingers from the throttle position. That's the kind of thing you do when you're twenty-six and an idiot.

Somewhere along the way, Julie sold me her Falcon station wagon. It had a homemade rack on top, Montana plates, and no first or reverse gears. I drove it strategically, keeping an eye out for places I wouldn't have to back out of, preferably on downhill slopes. I kept the car like that for a long time. It reminded me of her.

KATE LAKE

The Queen's Cadillac

I lived in a studio apartment in a building of gay men. My neighbors Chuck and Ken liked to perform in drag shows downtown. Chuck was a big guy, maybe 6 feet and 250 pounds. In chiffon and full wig, he was epic. Ken was Chuck's escort and he drove the pride of the Blackstone Apartments garage: a '74 Cadillac El Dorado convertible. It was aqua and had white upholstery and a bad valve tap. Sometimes all the tenants would gather in the lobby to see them off to a competition—waving as we watched Chuck's feather boa wafting from the front seat as they drove away. Once, they had a big fight and Ken emptied a gallon of barn-red exterior semigloss paint all over the Cadillac. It was really depressing to see that car after that.

1962 Ford Ranchero

A baby-blue cowgirl Cadillac with a phone dial where the horn used to be.
Like the Falcon before it, it had come from Montana. I bought it for $100 from
a graphic designer who had used it to haul his portfolio around. The phone dial
honked, but only if you dialed Operator. My relationship with Julie, tempestuous
from the get-go, ended when I met Rick. I used the Ranchero mostly to move.
Rick had a big book habit and a nomadic lifestyle. We moved his books almost
six times in the course of our relationship. As pathologies go, book collecting is
relatively harmless until it exceeds the room one can afford to house the habit.
We moved from a studio apartment to a one-bedroom to a two-bedroom, until
we were forced to look for permanent exhibition space in the form of a house.
Eventually the Ranchero, made for toting around hay and attending monster
truck rallies, not for the heavy lifting of the intelligentsia, died.

KATE LAKE

Toyota Land Cruiser

In 1983 I took a trip to Nicaragua. They had had a little revolution; it sounded like some cool things were happening. I didn't realize that they were also at war. One day, we were invited to go to *la frontera*. We bundled into a Toyota Land Cruiser and spent twelve wrenching hours navigating roads-in-name-only, fording rivers next to ruined bridges, and finally arriving at a sad little town on the border. The people there seemed shell-shocked. An old woman followed us down the street pleading for "aspirin, or valium, anything to stop the sound of the bombs." The Land Cruiser sat parked in the muddy plaza like a spaceship waiting to take off once its pale, alien riders had re-boarded. We traveled back in silence. At one point we had to quit the road altogether because it looked like it had been mined. Whenever I see Land Cruisers parked in front of nice restaurants or the mall, I think about the old lady.

1976 Volvo Sedan

The eighties were a blur of heterosexuality and career advancement. I don't know if the two things were related. Rick and I dated, moved in together, got married, and bought real estate. After the Ranchero went to the junkyard, I bought a 1976 light-gray Volvo with medium-gray vinyl upholstery and loose steering. I'm not sure if it was possible to find a more boring car. I drove it for a year or two, until I realized that getting into that car every morning was contributing to a growing problem with depression. I started to see a therapist who agreed I should lose the Volvo. I sold it to a man who "wanted something safe for his wife."

God is in the Detail

My sister and brother-in-law, Jim, lived in Southern California. Saturday
afternoon in their neighborhood was carwash time. Guys hauled out the
detergent and chamois and whitewall polish and carnauba wax and had at it.
Sometimes a game was on, blasting from the garage, and there was usually
a cooler of brew nearby. Jim took Q-Tips to his wheels. He had a Toyota truck
that sat real high on oversized tires and a jacked-up suspension. His vanity plate
said CUBS FAN. A few years after he got it, my sister gave him a license-plate
holder that added: NOT CUBAN. He's just a dude from Kentucky and got tired
of people pulling up beside him at stoplights and yelling about Castro.

1986 Honda Civic Hatchback

I got a management job and a Honda in the same week. To get to my job, I drove the Honda through miles of suburbs, to an office park sitting on what had once been wetlands. From my office I could watch flocks of migrating birds circle in confusion until they alighted, exhausted, on the parking lot. The first few times I saw this I wept. We bought a house in a transitional neighborhood. It came with rose bushes and fig trees. When the next round of funerals came—my father and grandparents—I had a husband to lean on. I was learning to let myself be a weepy fool. Rick was a sweet man, but sometimes, when it all got a bit much, I would put on my shades and drive the Civic slowly past one of Seattle's girl bars, sneaking glances at the cute little baby dykes loitering around outside.

KATE LAKE

Tank Half Empty in Singapore and Other Crimes

My job took me to Asia occasionally. My contact in Singapore was a guy named Sri who liked to dress up in vaguely female attire and was obsessed with Richard Gere. We spent a lot of time together. He had a little Korean car, a Daihatsu or something. He was nervous about the car. Singapore had a lot of car laws and Sri was breaking many of them. One is: You can't let your gas tank be less than half full. It's a $500 fine. A lot of things in Singapore carry $500 fines. Failure to flush a toilet, for example. Or driving between six and midnight on odd-numbered days. Sri needed to register his car (illegally) across the causeway in Malaysia, so one day we went there. On the way back he bought ten copies of the Richard Gere classic *Pretty Woman* and asked me to smuggle them back into Singapore for him. *Pretty Woman* was banned in Singapore. He felt they would recognize his car, but I could just walk through and, if I was caught, plead stupid tourist. By the time I reached the guard checking passports I was sweating bullets. I thought: Do I really want to go down for a Disney movie?

The Popemobile

I love the Popemobile. It looks like a cross between the AMC Pacer and a ride at Tomorrowland. I know the whole reason for the Popemobile is sort of sad, but it reminds me of those relics you see in old European cathedrals: the big toe of St. Thomas or the spleen of St. Theresa. Someone somewhere decided the pope was already a relic and he's been encased and put on display for believers and tourists alike.

Granddad's Skylark

My grandfather was the coolest man
I ever knew. He was a coal miner and
he worked in a lumberyard and he was
a medic in the war. He wasn't a wordy
guy but get him going and he could tell a
story that would make you laugh yourself
stupid. When he started having a hard time caring for
himself, I drove back to Oklahoma to stay with him for a week. He was sort
of confused. One night I heard him crashing around in the living room and when
I went downstairs and turned on the light, he was sitting on the couch trying to
get his tool chest open. It was about 4:00 A.M. and he wanted to go out to the
carport and change the oil in the Skylark. He was pretty sure that it had been more
than three thousand miles since the last oil change. My aunts had put the car up
on blocks months before when it was clear he probably shouldn't be driving.

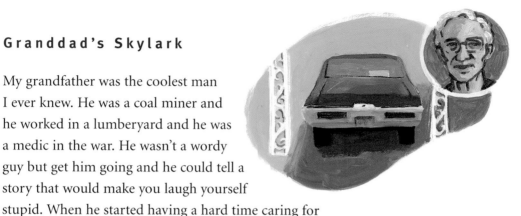

Public Transportation

After ten years of marriage, Rick and I agreed to live in different cities. I sold the Honda and moved to New York. For the first time as an adult I had no wheels of my own. On weekends I amused myself by taking the subway to random stops, emerging from the depths into strange and interesting neighborhoods. When I worked late at my job I was chauffeured home in a town car, an almost unbearable luxury. I fell back into the plush leatherette and watched the grated and graffitied storefronts of late-night New York slide past on my way back to my hovel in Brooklyn. Taxis were reserved for the occasional crosstown dash, visitors from out of town or late night respites from fear, fatigue, or weather. There were few sights more welcome on a cold, late night than an empty cab with its "vacant" light beckoning, offering shelter and the promise of safe delivery home.

Ford Contour

Rick and I met in London for a last whack at marriage saving. We rented
a car. We were hoping for an Aston Martin or a Vauxhall, but they only had
Ford Contours. The steering wheel was on the right side; our lane was on the
left. Rick drove first for about five minutes but he couldn't deal with a shrieking,
hysterical wife. I drove for the rest of the week. High in the Welsh hills, on
a windy country lane we found ourselves surrounded by sheep. Rick got out
to snap a picture of us. It's quite like a pretty postcard, except it was a Ford
Contour. It put both of us in peevish moods and we bickered through the
rest of the trip.

Jungle Jeeping

In San Jose, Costa Rica, my friend Linda and I rented a little Isuzu and promised solemnly not to drive it off-road. Two hours later we were grunting up a dry riverbed scattering large iguanas before us on our way to the mountains. Maybe we missed the main turnoff. It took us almost five hours to go thirty kilometers but when we reached the top and regarded the Pacific Ocean at our feet and the jungle before us, we felt victorious. For about five minutes. A diesel roar arose from the valley floor and soon a large and battle-scarred bus lurched over the horizon, DIOS MIO painted in large Gothic type on its front. It disgorged its passengers, a sixty/forty mix of locals and gringos, and then roared off to more remote outposts.

KATE LAKE

Betsy's Benz

My old flame Betsy moved to Berkeley, California, changed her name to Liz, earned an advanced degree, and bought a beautiful old Mercedes. At first things were tense between us. I judged her a yuppie and she felt judged. I visited her anyway and she let me drive her car, which was the excuse I needed to quit being such a pain in the ass. The Benz had polite little fins and an air of refined diplomacy. It was like driving around in an aging heiress. Outside a tony cheese shop it coughed and died. I was sure it had discovered what a plebeian I was and had opted to go no farther.

Dotcomobiles

I returned to the West Coast in 1994 to look into the Internet thing. I've always liked computers. They're sort of like cars, and there's an immutable logic to them—most of the time. I've never anthropomorphized my computers, though, never named one Nellie or stuck a dashboard Buddha to my monitor. I've never sat shivah outside a junkyard after selling a PC for scrap, like I did when the Ranchero died. I worked with a lot of young jocky geek-guys who obsessed about their rides. One bought a Miata and sold it three weeks later after his friends kidded him about driving a chick car. He bought an enormous SUV and took out most of the curb edging in the company lot. The president ran through BMWs like water, totalling two inside of six months. It became a badge of proletarian honor to drive a wreck. I kept the Honda.

In '95, my old friend Julie discovered she had breast cancer. Every week I drove over to her house and brought her little things: books, flowers, toys. I told her they were to remind her of beauty in the world but I was terrified of losing her, and the gifts comforted me most of all.

NASCAR

Some of my work buddies and I flew to Indianapolis for the Brickyard 400. I was doing some work for NASCAR and needed to get in touch with the stock-car aesthetic. The cars were Chevies and Dodges and Fords with bored-out, hopped-up engines. NASCAR has pretty rigid rules about things like valve-train weight and camshaft design and what you can and can't do to a car so it's a level playing field. You'd think with all that parity and a reasonably flat track, it would be boring. But when the flag drops and those big engines start growling up behind the pace car and the noise sweeps up over the grandstands and drowns out even the roar of the rabid fans, even the most jaded city girl can get a rush.

Subaru Wagon

In the middle of the last decade of the previous century, I met Mary. She was smart, beautiful, sexy, funny, and loving. She drove a beat-up old Toyota she called Beige-a Vu. The car/lust link that had applied to men thankfully played no role in my falling in love with her. She wanted to buy a new car and agonized over which make and model said "Mary." She loved station wagons but from ten feet away everything looked like a Nissan Sentra. She decided on a Subaru Wagon and bought a green one, which was promptly stolen and totaled. She bought a red one. So far, so good. We lashed kayaks and camping paraphernalia to the top and spent the first years of our relationship being outdoorsy. Whenever I see a red Subaru Outback now, my heart quickens while I scan for her familiar face and hair. How funny we should connect our lovers to these machines. Someone told me I should get a new car, that I'm not the Honda Civic type. They were right.

1966 Lada

My friend Teri went to Honduras to teach school and fell in with a couple of ex-pat Germans there. They shared a house in the hills above Tegucigalpa and a decrepit yellow Lada station wagon. The roads from their house to town were precipitous and poorly maintained, or maintained as well as roads in any poor neighborhood of a poor city. One morning a dog ran out in front of the Lada and in the ensuing confusion, the car flipped onto its roof and the three found themselves careening full tilt downhill upside down. Miraculously, they avoided hitting anyone on the crowded streets. They finally came to a stop in front of the public market. By the time they climbed out alive but bruised, a large crowd of onlookers had converged upon the car and stripped it clean.

Princess Diana Mercedes

I worked for a big national on-line news outfit for a while. I won't say which one—I think they're all about the same. My beeper went off just as I was leaving the movies one night. Princess Diana had been in a horrible crash. By the time I got to the newsroom, she was in the hospital but still alive and we had a logo: **Princess Di Crash.** There weren't many pictures on the wire yet, so we scanned the databases for maps of Paris and schematics of late-model Mercedes. When we found one, we created a diagram of the safety features in those cars. We put it on the Web, under a shot of the totaled car. The ad on the page was for Mercedes. It read, "When Life Is Good. . . ," or words to that effect. We tried all night but we couldn't get rid of the ad until the next day.

KATE LAKE

1998 Fiat Uno

Mary and I circumnavigated Sicily in a rented Fiat. We could have gotten a Ford Contour but the Fiat offered a degree of camouflage and clearly knew the terrain. I enjoy driving in places where people believe in Fate—usually Catholic or Muslim or Hindu countries. Negotiating strange streets, deciphering international road signs, being passed on the right at precipitous curves; it all becomes a contemplative exercise when one concedes will and the power to effect it. In Agrigento we parked and hiked a short hill to a massive Greek temple. The rock it was built on, some two thousand years earlier, was etched with fossil seashells from a long-gone ocean floor. I was beginning to understand that embracing what's next doesn't require discarding what has passed. When we walked back down to the parking lot, the Fiat's battery had died. Three laughing Italians gave us a push and we were on our way again.

I'm Driving a Stolen Car

My Civics kept getting stolen or broken into. When I got them back, and I always did (unfortunately), they never ran well again. One day my neighbor, who had made a fairly smooth transition from Scary Teenage Hoodlum to Leader of Tomorrow, explained that Hondas were the car of choice for street racing. A kid could steal it, do something clever to the carb, and then redline it, all in one evening. One particular gang was the chief perpetrator in our neighborhood. If you wanted to find your car quickly, you just needed to head toward the outlying boulevards at 3:00 A.M. until you heard the whine of Japanese engines in high distress.

Sometimes the cars were returned minus a few key parts, which meant another group was at work—stealing enough parts off enough cars to assemble a completely "new" car. I like to think the DNA of my cars is out there, disseminating.

Jim's Police Cars

Jim was a one-of-a-kind guy—a fisherman, a scrounger, a wheeler-dealer, an arts patron, an entrepreneur. The sort of person they just don't make a lot of anymore. He knew a good deal when he saw one so when he happened across an ad for a police auction, he was there, front and center. Somewhere toward the end of the auction, Lot 126 came up—twenty-one decommissioned police cars for an embarrassingly low sum. Jim did a little quick math and minutes later he was a proud fleet owner. Selling the cars was more problematic than he had anticipated—not many of his friends were wild about tooling around in police cars, decommissioned or not. But he dropped the price, and soon the city's impoverished struggling artists were driving 1982 two-tone Dodge Coronas, and the streets around local art openings looked like police actions.

Auto Dynamics in the 'Hood

My neighborhood was pretty interesting. There had been Italian families there since the twenties, and two Orthodox synagogues. There were immigrants from Southeast Asia and the Horn of Africa and Russia and Croatia. There were Samoans who played cricket in the park and drove tricked-out vans, and gay families with houses full of children and Ford Windstars. There were good ol' boys and Boeing workers and old hippies of every color, unemployed dotcommers, and a little storefront church called El Luz del Mundo where Charismatics from Mexico formed a community. There were a lot of old Volvos and they seemed to cross class and race lines. Newcomers to the country liked upscale generic cars—Acuras and Lexi if they could afford them. A lot of the kids, black and white, liked sharkers: beat-up seventies cruise-mobiles like Chrysler New Yorkers and Mercury Marquis. Southeast Asian kids seemed to like Hondas and BMWs with stuffed animals in the rear window. There were lucky-rich techies with new Saabs, and bubbas with Wranglers. It was a damn global village.

Kids

A lot of the children that used to play tag on my lawn are teenagers now, with their own wheels. There's a lot of brake squealing, engine revving, and slow trolling with seats so low and ratcheted back the cars look like unpiloted drones. The anointed ride shotgun and everyone else fights for back seat windows. Romance and territorial defense translate into abrupt acceleration, honking, and the overt display of unnecessary accessories like car bras and spoilers. On dark side streets, their cars idle quietly, and through the tinted glass, you can make out their silhouettes. Maybe they're getting high or having sex, but mostly I figure they're just hanging out in the car.

1968 Three-Quarter-Ton Chevy Pickup

I justified this for hauling compost and other household detritus, although I actually don't do a lot of that. Mostly I just saw myself as a girl who should have a truck. Silly and environmentally incorrect, but there you have it. I bought this honker on the Internet from a retired Boeing engineer. It's immaculate. When I registered it, I discovered it had "collector" plates. I asked the girl behind the counter why a 1968 truck would be a collectible and she tells me it's because it's an antique.

1985 Jaguar XJ-6

My neighbor Gerald found a beautiful but decrepit, ivy-engulfed old Jag in a backyard out in the sticks. He got it for a song and handed it over to a guy he knew who could restore it to its former luster. The restorer was thorough and it took a long time. About four years into it, he had a religious awakening and refused to return the Jag until Gerald went to church with him. Gerald eventually had to break the Eighth Commandment and steal his car back.

Julie is six years past her diagnosis now and doing well. She got the other nipple pierced. Rick is married again and happy. Sean lives on fourteen acres of Oregon pastureland dotted with old bikes. When we all get together we marvel at the years that have passed, the way we can toss off the fact we've been friends for twenty-five, thirty years. That we roamed the world, or fell in love, divorced, fought cancer, or bore and raised children. That we have traveled away from each other and have returned, changed and the same.

2001 Audi Quattro TT

The past few years have been good ones. I've been lucky and blessed. It's high time for a decent midlife-crisis car. The TT is pure porn: All-wheel drive. 225 hp turbo. Stainless-steel dash and Bose sound. Out on the interstate, I took it to 120 without really trying. It has six gears but I think the sixth is just a promise more than anything. When I go fast like that, something that feels like ecstasy wells up. It's a conspiracy between me and this great thrumming engine to see what we're capable of. Around town I feel guilty, as if I'm keeping a great beast contained. When I park it, I'm reluctant to leave. Men are openly envious. They say, "How do you like it?" knowing damn well what the answer will be. Women, when they say anything, say, "Can you really see out of that thing?" They probably think I'm an asshole.

KATE LAKE

Parts Warranties

I suppose I thought we'd all be driving little jet mobiles by now, not SUVs
and minivans. The future has surprised me with its recalcitrances as well as its
advances. I rarely look under a hood anymore; there's not much reason. All the
components are vacuum-packed and stashed away from nonprofessional tool
users. There's no great pride in the ability to rattle off the names and numbers
of great engines. The 328, 235, slant-six. The V-8. Knowing what a universal joint
does is no longer central to getting one's feminist creds. Most guys I know are the
same way and it's no surprise. The cupholder really is more relevant to our lives.

Sometimes at night, though, I'll hear an engine coming over the hill, down
the street. It has a rumble that I know has something to do with custom carbs
and greasy fingernails. It sounds like teenage sex and road trips and freedom.
It sounds illicit. It sounds good.

Postscript

I see it on the street here and there. A red 1965 Citroen DS19. It usually has a good-looking brunette at the wheel. She always seems to be in a hurry or on an errand. In some past life, I knew that car. Maybe I was in Paris or Africa. Maybe I was having an argument with a lover when it tore past and disappeared into traffic. Or I turned my head and thought I saw it. I've never driven one, but there's plenty of time.

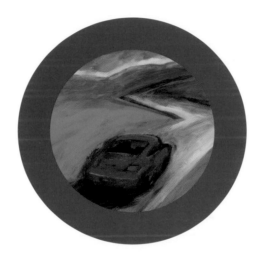